nature felt but never apprehended

nature felt but never apprehended

Angela Peñaredondo

NOEMI

Published by Noemi Press, Inc. A Nonprofit Literary Organization. www.noemipress.org

Cover Image: Marigold Santos, *Sublimation* 2017, 108" x 156" Acrylic and pigment on canvas. Courtesy of the Artist. Photography by Charles Cousins, courtesy of the Art Gallery of Alberta.
Cover & Book Design by co·im·press

ISBN: 978-1-955992-01-5

to maria luz and virginia and their mothers and their mothers' mothers . . .

contents

naked · strategic · partners

to · hold · these · contradictions · in · kinship

In the revolutionary movement, such surplus can be found in the form of surplus life that is produced through rituals of radicalized grief and the invocation of what I call divine sorrow …

—Neferti X. M. Tadiar

I did arise from
        tenderness: I touched
            not: I silvered
                love.

—José García Villa

[mercy ceremony]

i am slaying you   in my dreams   no slaying you for reals this time

steel pointed aimed like hawk bone at your bare collar   your eyes tell

of those once-privileged limbs   that mouth that consumed everything it could because it believed
it could with even knowing the immensity

what was stripped away from me is no longer an invisible assault buried under bladed tendrils of seaweed
havoc of sea grapes there's nothing holding me back from carving as one does when whittling wood

this butterfly blade on soft tissue to etch my name   on your skin this name for ocean its secret wind
this tender gouge   jellyfish all cinematic haunting above flaring sea anemones

1

black sands of my birth its unseasonable foam   you rope-bound covered in lava sediment i set your
weight on a raft just made for your tied up frame burn guava leaves above each part

                                                                           stamped in volcanic ash

i hover longer over bandaged eyes wrinkled genitals moistened pod now waiting to return to the
undulating underbelly   blow smoke into your one exposed ear so you can feel my life force
one last time

like intentional stars colliding   as i push your raft off   into what's destined to consume

confrontations·earth·ephemera

[dear tree, dear shrapnel...]

dear tree, dear shrapnel radio wire, and tacloban, where you carried cement-filled rice sacks on your back each knucklebone swollen, two hands clasping

a childhood story of your cousin who left home at fifteen from the town of dueñas about her mother who smoked too much shabu at night, wallowing in opprobrium

feminization of wage labor tells me *house home domine domina* to create work and sensation as fragrant as plumeria, their ivory petals with a sunlit center, and us

[central visayan mountain range]
philippines, 1945

when hiding from enemies

               at least one dream away from machines & from bodies
that do not sleep he drags his thumb along his lover's smudged chin & notices his face bathed & earthen

the trees once giants, are giants again he tells the moon *they come savage and without undoing*

after a grenade falls a fresh cavity in the ground appears as a nest and he wishes his own children
might forget him   they will be the lucky ones   to live   enemies must believe him gone

they are not from these caves dear santos dear virgen evoke what luz perpetual dear palmettos &
saltwater be all & his mouth too

his lover lies down wet ground speaking only what he knows dripping face the shrapnel moon
he whispers his want   to dissolve like this in ferns

[survivor's topography]

like an upward buttress a gaur skull & her horns calls in evidence at the walls of a catholic church
skeleton :: coral of aklan :: contractual object

coffers horizontal & hanging   ask what signage occurs as schemata for rescue   oars that lifted
a boy out of floods   its plains a site of anticolonial experience

in direction of what now possesses you   i pray at 2.5 meters above sea level   children
    astral renegades   reverence for labor expands with untranslated vocabulary

contour through union of mountains   confusion of phragmites
a divine missive   brown scales of flesh   water :: measure for haunting
                                        what need   needs not saving

before birth rivulets   wonderment of bones splayed out like numerology across
                an eroded altar   of   geo me   try

solitude & work merge   offer a bed   of moss & teak bark from this submersion
somewhere in these militarized lands   there are rivers   nets

there are   before my birth   bodies you cannot see
                from this excavated   map   made   &   unmade

[letter to streets that burned you]

dear (un)given name
      one-who-has-been-heard
      if tied by rope
      if paired with glass
      if adorn in tektite

dear sunburst of whipped black wigs
      emerald sari starlets
      at the tsubaki nightclub
      on the corner of mabini street

dear manila at dawn
      ask the soldiers why
      they imprisoned them in barracks
      now the rizal memorial
      sports complex

dear golden gays of pasay
          you know what's god-like
          sugarcane field dandies
          bitter melon bakla
          queens in violent eye shadows

dear bar girl in a fish tank
          nipple fringes rage
          to swaying hosannas
          pinwheel earrings shine
          as still-empty hands cup

dear minerva, carmen, and sophie
          barnyard death before sunlight—
          they cut grass on their knees
          gatherers of their own hair
          applaud their femme bodies
          anoint them where they lie

dear black market healer
    even blindfolded—you're much
    more than others realize
    fingers clasping shape
    of infinity but someone
    made you believe
    mouth's   the limit

[exigencies in layers i]

sediment:
attacker, interrogator, ungrateful & exorbitant
you do not end with age

sediment:
to vanquish
one's crucial identity

partial lithification:
tell me what it means to view this body outside
of a fetishized object
or extinction

sedimentary rock:
mattresses split in two

shale:
when your body is not yours to own
concrete and finite without
guidance from the sun

sedimentary conglomerate:
you are farther from me now
even when i flee or fight off
flashes, you simply desire me awry

breccia:
love us in our deviancy
fossil of hope

[exigencies in layers ii]

cuticle:
    can you be your own mirror your naked privilege the earth floor in shadow

upper epidermis:
    who is your realized self when hurt or hunted

epidermal hair:
    birdsong renders to tiny explosions   in the veins of pacific archipelagos

substomatal chamber:
    if you want to transform me then sacrifice

palisade mesophyll:
  when was the last time mother   you loved yourself   before others   before you
  abandoned   yourself for men   before you washed & scrubbed backsides
                                         of these monolithic   structures

that collapse   your vascular   bundle   sheath   mother
  in disaster   we ask perpetually

xylem:
  should have been you father father these sediments father droplets of giving mist
                  father winged & wingless   father wants   father notice us
        father failure   father sonic surface alone

  father without sunlight you   decay

air channel:
  pressure evolves a range of   shock is no longer in me

guard cells:
    collective praying hands

stoma (pore):
    exist   to exhibit   imperfections   of men   of institutions   of church
        those senescent pathologies that assume the form of tradition

air channel:
    ask me what i want

phloem:
    ask me what i need

chloroplasts:
    what is your method of asking?

lower epidermis:
    the fighting invisible   resistant ghosts   shapeshifters
               who alchemize   who enable
               words & ash   unremitting   counter-meanings

[trace]

fire ants carry a loaf of living—a portrait emerges as survival circuit
our grandfather's father's father could not forge   what was not permitted

after so much rupture this portrait is only an imprint

after rusted blades   transfigure to fine alluvial dust

site of reclamation   even before articulation of futurity from a single photograph
                            of our infancy

before occupation   of adulthood this story is real
                          this story is real

this resistance story about young bodies   double helix &
time travel on the sea   watch us come back   as orbs floating

[nights you go trembling]

there are nights you go trembling in this condition / cracked & pried open like a holiday crab / hoof marks
of your great-grandfather's carabao / visions below ground / malunggay branches ember /

your ripped up / letters morph to moths / white crackle of gmelina wood / summon grief from sub-caldera
/ endangered indigenous pine /

    narra / akle / supa / almon / yakal / vatica elliptica / children came

into this world angry / leapt from shaggy rooftops / apprehended / without documentation / it took years
to get their names back / to have them spelled /

praise aloud spatter of lovely surnames / of sisters from the same barrio / from unwanted touch / passed
dilapidated halls & fields / worship fueled by condemnation / no reparations made / by empire or industry

incognito / playing out / in dream-maps full of x's / sting at the script / simply that's the way things are

[on cures & abrasions from a responsive environment]

what was once wild   chicken & pig farms   once hectares of pineapple fields
banana   coffee   cacao   rice   corn   now inedible   unlivable density

from village to village she tramples   her land extends beyond parameters
    families & homes washed by volcanic dust

    it rains like this   in abundance   into her briny tinctures   futurity & ashfall bond
in her throat   concepts   from the survivor   blast after blast

    chopped   burned portions of earth
    shelter an architecture   of fallen switches   from her hands

herbs   she rinses in taal's ruined lake   if not from the violence of water
then fire   *capitalism, having already found a way to turn profit on disaster*

      she formulates   teleportation devices   out of root bark   what empire identifies as poor
as poor   as docile   does surveillance mean the same as command?

         remember what it's like   to be of this deserving place
she continues to scan   for any of the living birds
                  through the barrel of a sugarcane stalk

technology against incendiary epistemes   she wipes down the fevered
               makes what's bruised aromatic

of those once-privileged limbs that mouth
that consumed everything it could because
it   believed   it   could
with   even   knowing   the
i   m   m   e   n   s   i   t   y

the·dead·teach·living

[meditations on a fist]

1.

clenched foot is to a body-object that strikes with fists around a wooden rod or slippery metal
    that pushes heavy hooves through a field's shallow rainwater I grew around acres of mud
    and the seeds we planted under its weight

fist equivalent to machete   as rifle   as beretta   as pistol
above a skull   opens into a plume

all five fingers can fit into womb or mouth
    a man seated tied with hemp rope a strung-up rooster
    eyes wide to the ivory

names & coordinates he confesses once a fist is removed
rain stops and heat rises to ten

2.

i cannot recall how early i knew or how it was shown to me as a girl in my mother's parlor
the piano the mahogany floor smelling of wet earth fingers elongated to each personality

legs crossed in a schoolyard my hands folded like gowns over my lap

open open open

old woman slices an okra's tawny root a fish laid out glassy and gutted i clutch meat and foliage
cutting with precision and speed   i cannot keep up my own fingers   i cannot help but
          cut   yes the fist
                                        i can speak more   on slicing

3.

as a comet   curls to meet the invisible rendering them quiet
         cannot fit into this mouth but teeth get in the way

men have named me small said my cavity is not equipped to protect me learned this first from my
mother that night i dreamt of pummeling
         a man to paint
                          how to break his nose
without breaking my fist first

             then there's a gift above all gifts   this nautilus of skin
i can make love with it   talk into an endless   with or without grief

[transmitter signals when in proximity to power collapse]

his clicking mouth like morse code his slippers slap across the hard wood floor of our house his country that is his militarized body.

the untouched plate rice and dried fish banana sliced with a spoon he paces in his underwear white ribbed tank torn at the seams a gold medallion with words

deus, deus, deus

form an obtuse triangle unguarded between throat & breastbone how to not conjure the stones but heat itself.

from his lips   licks salt and earth.

after a loved one dies, their spirit lingers for nine days. this means nine days of prayer, nine days the spirit walks through the house flicking light switches, blowing out altar candles.

a kitchen clock lands on the dead's lucky number. on breakfast dishes, papaya seeds glance back like opals.

their song plays on a device at sundown. jasmine, amber, and burnt wax in a mirrorless room.

    clinging earth in your thumbnails
    read the dirt as a cast

    hunger : rain :: fever : black stone

sleep does not arrive because of our dead but of   love for our dead.

he originates to apparition
at the end of the hall, examines borders

of a wall mirror expecting to find a hidden   switch to a trapdoor.

                              once his reflection de-
                                    territorializes

a clearing appears before him.

through silt and its rhizomes, he runs

through sacramental mounds until feet,

breasts, arteries, and joints unfix

& feather.   he sprints

into a future. throat carries

the 3,700 seed capsules

he will regurgitate to mush,

nursing outstretched mouths.

[to dream of a cardinal feeding . . .]

to dream of a cardinal feeding

        a shiny fish head resurfacing from the acidic peat.

        imagine an orange beak and a protrusible mouth, kissing.

to dream of a red-crested

        cardinal inside some kind of henhouse.

        there's a big fire.

        there is a matchbook in my hands.

it is afternoon and thirsty as his hands wrestle her against the kitchen counter i remind him again that he knows her even as he shakes.

her head and throat
a ripe guava before it falls.

years later, when I'm no longer a child, i throw a hot cup at my lover's feet. this is how
i learned not to beg   then a jar of yellow carnations.

i'm told over and over that i must be crazy. it's a week before what this country proclaims independence day and our apartment windows wide to a season of wildfires, hillside oak torched to pin cushions.

on the brown carpet, i succumb. i remind myself i can love

but i'm told it's hysteria.

to dream of snakes

there is a box i want to seal them in

their glossy corneas, dagger

tongues shifting mettle

there is an open box i cannot seal

i conjure a blade to ravage open   a bigger container

[ghosts in charged objects]

dear ghosts hiding in charged objects and blood stories

who did you cut out years ago?

all these predictions in the parlor

in paramilitarism   in a hidden battle   140,000 women

handgun   rifle   long gun   long shot

m1 carbine   bolo   butterfly to blades   forged   all redolent

picture diary of a girl   *girllll*   *gurl*   *grrrl*   *grrlzz*

grease gun   browning   m1911   1918   1919 garand grand   grandiose   glorious   gluttonous   geographic   gratuitous

inventory of suppression

[becoming a minke whale]

underwater, she endures. attempts to create a viable future in shifty green among other whores and feminists. akin to frilled sharks in cabaret, the angler in grotesque horniness, her obsessions over hairy antennae oscillating in the dark.
above, parties of war continue. on land, what's there to need? mud, stools. the salacious heat.

certainly, she has mended enough quilts and cotton to comfort her lover's body during late rough nights. no more rice or pickled singkamas or the goat knuckle stew that she fed the soldiers in their heavy boots—who stole all her spoons and pretty effigies, their mouths stuffed with porridge and belly meat.

let her have ocean. gargantuan, iridescent cunt kaleidescoping to the black sea.
map. clock. contract. kill. they all mean something different down here.

she'll gulp oysters and mussels down with no desire for palm wine. she'll read books, floating on her side, spectral algae tickling her brain and wanted curvy fat. in that unreachable sky some human might describe as precious or turquoise, she knows paradise lives elsewhere.

black   sands   of   my   birth

its   unseasonable   foam

you   rope-bound   covered

in   lava   sediment

[tattoo as softening ritual]

a healer lifts a burning bowl of copal, touch its edges to their forehead as they tell me of when
they lived in the global south. curanderas mistook them for their local indigenous woman.
chestnut skin, wide noise dignified like aspects of their shaved head.
they chant behind smoke of gold resin.

in the philippines, ancestors burned native copal from the agathis dammara tree,
now endangered.   tree gum holds a history of forest collecting:

bone   bird   insecta   fur   leaf   pod   wing venation

media. costa. radius. crossvein. cubitus. jugal.

sap—an archive.

it's the first day of a new year

a tattoo doula holds my skin taut   while the healer angles each poke and prod

in such a way   to feel each stride of needle fully   tradition

to wail   ritual   what curiosity to witness its embodiment

like a moment some star releases itself from dark   unclutched

from its trapeze   of mess and tangle

scarifications on their back marble to gliding lizard   my breasts

graze scales   lizard is eaten by another

what was charred was once hungry

a slow needle conjures storm   in a state of acute listening

an infusion of fire one layer at a time

to honor suffering

voices speak in tongues   approaches a doorway ajar

          then weight beside a pillow

what do you do when all your parts bring fire

my trapped voice fires loudest

          searing gale trapped inside a skull

i see a man's face   painted white cloth   when I wake everything in me tremors

                  shattering

                      in all directions

demons have their own style of curating pain

they yank out dried   spiny branches covered in clusters of ants   do you see

        where my body

      dissolves then archives

alongside moist herbs water paired with blood ritual

like the lesser wax moth who breeds life in abandoned
unoccupied spaces of what was

fossilized in tree gum   this grief in trance

narratives generated inside colonies

of bone require
submission

then an asphyxiation   my breath collapses out of implosion   falling

when i get up   another unexposed world

i uncover what has not been killed   like dyed linen dripping on a line   absent of a body

i hang what has survived   produced underneath wet ground matter

inside a pit
i inscribe mythology

yearning of sky   from a boat   an empire aflame

these poems not old enough
                        to fade into afterlife

angels know nothing   of angels

unrecorded utters   vocal hymns

        harmony   terrible   harmony

        i dig   to break an imperial house

give light to this head arched upward   fire sings through the only hole in the room

        light sings through the only hole in the room

    some animals
   i recognize   i ask ancestors to recover their names
       it is here where some of them hunt

my brother holds my hand   reminds me of reconciliation   on an altar

     one faded photo of us atop a precolonial cerulean city

         ripened pineapple
         deck of playing cards
         bottle of coconut oil
         centipede incased in a plastic cube
         crossing one world to the next on 177 legs

my openings brew divination   overgrowth in glass jars   heavy bracts the size of paws

i weave geranium & aloe   water an atlas of spaciousness

mere shrubs sprout into age   like a rubber plant lumbering over mallows   to become

                              eaten rainfall for the deities

disproportionate but abundant

                    i dream of wrapping four
                    snakeheads in burlap
                    to be brought back home

naked·strategic·partners

i set your weight on a raft just made for your tied
up frame burn guava leaves above each part
stamped in volcanic ash

i

hover
hover

[a girl too disenchanted to indulge in romantics]

her body a tiny lake
on the tabletop
fingers of sticky rice
she eats with
clouds craves
nothing else
mashing them
to impermanence
the kitchen always
smells of jarred rain
and silver ghosts

powders her face to almost-snow
porcelana that's what her mother
calls it (right kind of sheen) there's
no time to stay (herself) she has
a prized date   it is night in a
vacant parking lot (open trunk of
a car) what she steals she smokes
slow as *ruffled skirts that raise*
themselves (like a phantom ship)
on a sea of oil she presses a glass
                    bottle to lips
                    conquest
                    of sugarcane
                    tanduay-dark with
                    the gold seal

with some friends at a bar her tailbone in
triangulation with a hard angle of light (in
halogen red) she sits underneath a print of
paula rego's painting
*snow white playing with her father's
trophies* (obedient and defiant)   lap
in charmeuse between severed animal
heads (antlers upward like branches)
smiling she signals the bartender with a
nod (for the bill) another one for prosperity

at a window seat of a moving bus (or a train) flash
of a movie screen (hidden) suggests easy pleasures
of pale flesh indignantly she turns away looks out
the window an (indecipherable) sheath of
phosphorescence beams across her forehead
(sterling mise en abyme) as the locomotion
accelerates then faces (like ash) pans & pans
    where's the sandbar
its driftwood   discarded
    cold claws   still full of fights

inside an expensive restaurant knives and soup spoons dip in fatty omegas over a phone call she convinces the other how adoration will go (like this broth) and sacrifice (a reunion of adventures) a body's departure (not made of or from crust or callous) the voice on the receiving end replies *that's how you ended up with a bundle of medicine in that sweaty hole i mean the dense woods i mean into a bright monster made of jungle fowl*

her palms rotate a planet until the milk of a young coconut rivers   there are
other meanings here for god for mahogany mud rife in the tropics   its withs or
withouts   but the ordinary crack of exo   a green head shields a smaller
brown one then punctured against a sharp thing with one blow
do not think of sex or the usual   think of a mild smashing
experienced hands on a precise split

                                        to smell the buried
                      trembling
                                 requited jelly

[cut an opening to mend the me]

how must one proceed toward potential? when splintered enough, boiled down to transparent bits rendered invisible, seen as commodity.

the body and this word as a cast spell, not separate from politics of biology.   this word meant for temple, land, safehouse, haven, archive, storage of data.

rendered indefinite if not mixed, blended thoroughly with pageantry of whiteness.

we are no longer seeking for the hard kind incapable of elasticity, but porous enough to release.

desire for home has attachments that deal little with real estate.

        diasporic embodiment is leaving for what-can-be-known.

exile is a river   at the end   a waterfall or delta.

        citizen or foreign   visitor with longing song   harana for

        the assemblage   circuitous   homing device.

        suspension & assimilation with a distant border in view

or lack—   *product of moonlight as much as sunlight.*

at midnight, i flip through old political cartoons from a giant book, rummage through family photos, then
watch filipino neo-realist films   from brocka, del mundo, bernal, raya martin . . .

lodged between fragments of memories and war stories my family kept hidden.
self-narration only goes so far.

from a letter, sent to me more than ten years ago, the writer explains: *reimagination and subversion*
should be inherent in any filipino work given our history. i am surprised when folks try to abide by the normative.

if assimilation is erasure, then survival is innovative.   queer and diasporic filipinx
bodies been seen as
reproduction . . . .   fetish…   anachronism . . .   unqualified good…

dislocation inevitably leads to adapting a praxis of forgetting.   but with forgetting comes
reimagination—hybridity of diasporic queerness.   materializes as polyphonic quiver as

                          korlong
                          as zither
                          as harp
                          as dystopian
                            lyric.

to classify as anything but singular is an intervention, a bridge between migration and when
trauma exposes the hybridity of the self, it exposes the multiple, often
incompatible . . .

tala oliver mateo's *carbon copies* was a series of long panels (identical in size) made of cosmetic foundation and peel-off masks.

the four colors represented were "nut brown/cocoa," "mutt," "nude beige," and "toast/hale"
tala arranged the panels from left to right, darkest shade to lightest shade, hung side-by-side, three feet apart. i observe the panels' thinness, their plasticized sound.

i wondered if they would melt from the salt of my hands, stain my fingers. before reaching out to them, i wiped the oil from my palms along my pant leg. i was surprised how they felt   durable
            like latex   an android . . .

sashed to alienation   ensemble set apart from normative   but in the dark   in the dark
jettisoned   *roots stalks and trees and then*   deviant thoughts and myself

i have not yet sung as i want   mine   *are*   *queer*
songs but as i get older   *they get queerer still*   as   survivor   *i*   *shall*   *write*
stranger songs   separate from my own body   consequentially my body's a book

ghost   ghoul   jovian   venusian   warm and soft out
without cohesion   subversive social commentator   *arbiter of culture*
i have learned to be lonely   *and stronger around these men*

tala the artist shows me a picture of a half-naked, muscular brown man on grindr. we chew on asparagus sandwiches. she tells me her memories of growing up in a military-dependent family, living all over: germany, hawaii, plains of the midwest. we scroll through dick pics and chat about how societal concerns associated to skin is feminized. how the feminine and skin obsession are synonymous. our mouths hover above our cups. her lips part just enough. cream in my earl grey sinks, turns the liquid from brown to nude beige.

tongue   tea   silks   when swallowed.

what is   the *the*   that separates us from desiring   ourselves?

viewers were encouraged to engage with the materiality of tala's flesh-colored panels, finger their way through them. sewing shears were left on a podium as instruments.

of engagement as interlocutor: the two middle panels were trimmed around
their edges by someone. soon after a few more snips from scissors, a bystander no longer a bystander
tied together two panels at their corners as if this counterfeit flesh held.

bonded by tails of braided hair. drapery of fake latex. mutt hooked with nude beige.

my mother and her mother
and her grandmother
told their children, mostly
daughters, not to stay out

for fear of the sun

for fear of their skin

for fear of a darkening

there was much caution when
scissor   blades   touched
toast/hale, the lightest of the
series of faux skin.
                    delicate slashes

like pixie cuts   i place on my tongue.
  do not look for cut thread.

    instead, give her a new identity.
    i give her the name
    primula vulgaris.

there was only half left of brown/cocoa.   someone cuts a rigid hole into

in the shape of a spade, frayed edges.

power of touch as both boundary and trespass

a diamond was cut out in the lower right quadrant.

in the lower left, a loin

and a big fat heart reclined, as if resting on its side.

[transmitter signals when in proximity to a hole]

the beginning starts like this, darwin said. let me say that it starts as a hole in the ground. no mystique as to why it's there. small metal or plastic pail of still water posted nearby. squatting anytime, all the time over this humble hole.

her name: jennifer laude. on the internet you can find almost anything. like a photograph of jennifer's trans filipina body. not soft burial linen but a white hotel sheet, wrapped around her. legs and arms exposed. a spongy cattail growing downward into a hole of a white toilet.

no need for these kinds of holes in north america, terrain of brave porcelain. cold & hard. through its round opening everything goes with speed, summoned away with no possibility of return.

north america, may your white toilets, eternally elliptical, stay en masse. not all formerly colonized countries use holes for shitting. there are some toilets too. for instance, in the big city in the philippines, toilets all the time . . .

how to shit the american way.
his name: joseph scott pemberton.
private first class pemberton, he tells
the press. he tells the court. he tells
jennifer's mother that he didn't know

jennifer was jennifer. he didn't know.
did not know her. know did not.
not did he know.
this much he knows.

i will tell you again:
there's a white hole with
a brown throat folded
in half—

make her a crown of
irises and cattails
offer her linen
as pall for veneration
her legs and arms:
whole

[transmitter signals when in proximity to overturning domestic imagination]

combustion from displacement
    borders dislocate a foot over

      heat only within the ribs' marker
    red bleeds to orange as if the jungles of the tropics collapse to an ultraviolet wave

                        another way war &
                        invisibility disco
                        inside me

    miniscule particles of disruption
gladiolas in a thousand funerary marches

                        nature exposes a crescendo
                        when we allow ourselves
                        the final feel of our enormities

penumbral
lunar eclipse
migrant bird = fire = brain matter

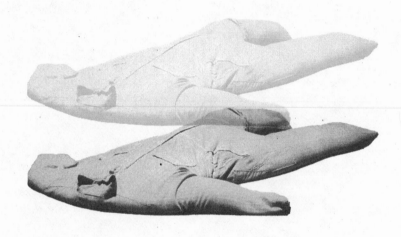

[keeper of blades]

she transforms into a keeper of blades, a herald of salt and bread stacked like sagada's
hanging sepulchers.

> egg-shaped heirloom of black pearls, pollen from calla
> lilies pock the mantle. her handsome head turns thorny,
> shattering her family's fine plates on a polished floor:

> pins marks on a pomelo tree, silver brocade of a visayan leopard
> holds an anger that hates moderation.

she wants something she's told she shouldn't have. her husband does not articulate this
but shows how his kind of freedom was not designed for her. so she keeps naming what
intercepts between her window and the noise in her head:

> rainbow eucalyptus,
> brandy, cassava,
> jade earring, a servant,

a nurse, a teacher,
anna and the king of siam,
wicky-wacky-woo.

she smashes everything until fractures blur—   to be of the ruling-ruling class.

[ ]

electric wasps follow sweeping
sounds of bristles
from a spiked broom made
from midribs of gathered
palm leaves. at last, a chiseled
edge scrapes against teeth
of a rough surface.

[albularya]

Gina init nila ang balunggay kag yukalipto sa tasa nga tisa
gin tanyagan ako sang mapulapula nga   lipstik   ang tsaa siling nila

para sa akon uhaw kag maluya nga lawas   ang lipstik naga pahanumdom sa akon
nga ang kamatayon maski daw madulum   indi lang isa ka duag

ang tanan sa sulod sang balay nila naga panimaho sang lana sang lubi   dahon sang palma
nagakabit sa ibabaw sang dapog   mga damang sa
                                        banggerahan wala nagahulag daw mga estatwa

may langgaw sa ibabaw sang lamesa nga plastik
ang mga langaw nagalupad palibot sa garapon nga may unod nga kaong

ang akon mabaskog nga hampak makakulurog sang lawas kag makapauntat sang antos

upos sa baba
bunga sang buyo sa ila dila
nagakanta samtang nagapinta sang akon bibig
daw sineguelas

unod sang sineguelas nga Espanyol   ang mga Katsila nabihag sa mga bighalan nga
babaye kaanggid sang sa Bibliya   nasilakan ako sang espeho
kag gina tan-aw ko ang akon ngipon nga na mantsahan

sa ibabaw sining payag nga tiko   daw sirik sang isda nga makapugong sang bagyo
may higante   pero indi pinakadaku nga bitoon sa kalingatan
nag kambyo ang hangin:

isa ka tampok sang naga-aso nga basura
kag ginasunog ang dahon sang molave
dayon balik sa bitoon

to·hold·these·contradictions·in·kinship

[amulet for changing child]

dear lamplight, *osprey with that cry*
i fear of fading uncombed forests & un-
cultivated grass

who named us pygmies
of the pacific archipelago?

they've written too many cockroach epistemologies
where's the industrial flypaper?
i hope this bane has made
a wild tribe whore out of my blood

line as tactics
film satirical portrait
film barbaric camp
film the police

proximity perversions have been historicized
my people will eat your *celestial placenta*
we shall eat on lush leaves, molding pale meat into lump sums

[transmitter signals from a young brown feminist]

dear queer choreography   moro folkloric dance moves to madonna's
        like a virgin &   dear gay immigrant child raised in the 90's

        not to be mistaken for digital natives   who obsess over throwbacks
prince of bel air & metallic balloon pants   turned jungle asia monstera print

when gasoline was under a dollar   minimum wage $3.75   when dhs once split
            to form a three-headed beast   dear competition of high femme-ness

            wooden abanicos like knives   pair of jaunty sunbursts
stilettos not on the cover   of *the zaragozian*   but instead veiled in funerary

sunday chic   dear limbs of my women   so much drama de-centering
        comeuppance   dear archipelago swag

                techno versions   of diasporic appliqué
        didn't claim citizenship until 25   after years of   teenage nerddom

in wet n wild lips   teased bangs at junior high skating rinks
talent for slash carnival show   then puberty came like bobby brown's no prerogative

dear festival of another virgin   in black biker shorts   raptorial nails & slumber parties
ferris wheel lit over a soccer field   dear coarse summer grasses   church basketball courts

& radio hits on police brutality   dear you who question   who could live as a boy
as america's brown pop stars   in fake leather   art deco neck chains spelling out

your first girlfriend's nickname   their mohawk black hair
skin of cassia eyes like pizecua   dear self who ran far away

who could not be father's son   father's right mind   even with a penciled zorro stache
rolled cameo sleeves   wingtipped   taxi dance hall shoes

liberated sluts laugh   clasping your uncle's arm   like doves
creeping false holy   dear providence   under pressure   culture vultures

belly bulging   with trapped love   ancestral grief   saints of transmission
        kilig kweens to believe in   painted bisayan princes

poet haranistas unusual & rare   writing into existence
                pantheon of goddexxex

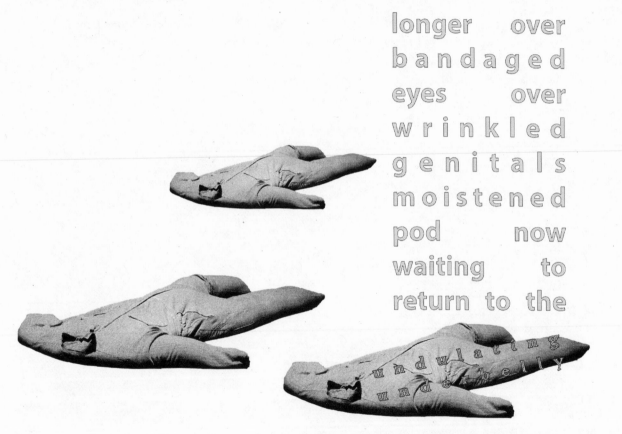

longer   over
b a n d a g e d
eyes   over
w r i n k l e d
g e n i t a l s
m o i s t e n e d
pod   now
waiting   to
return to the
undulating
underbelly

92

[contradictions in kinship]

forming an arrowhead, ibises carry each other in flight   in a direction i want to read
as a glyph of hope.

i walk east. a parking lot almost burns. the dusk's lukewarm to blush. then i'm back
again on the balcony of my university building six and half years before we met,
winds transporting brush sediments towards an approaching summer.

jacarandas and tolerant native vines. long auspicious walks on hot nights with a tuxedo
cat that seduced us, rolled her ass in dirt. under this sky, i nursed a kindling.

you feel gone more than ever. shoulders turning over in another bed. shadows
trespass my wilderness like ink spill, a reminder of those ibises,

of a secret set loose.   to pray for reckoning.

what gifts can i give my younger self?   the acacia that sprang
breaking through floorboards   of my childhood home on luna street

            father paid a local shaman to rid the tree's trunk
                            of its little evils.

i don't know if there's truth   in what they say
for regeneration to happen . . .

aerial roots dwindle on the ledge   while lightning and sand flay.

                wilder trees sell me
                safety but i ask
                my younger
                self

why they've been robbed   melancholy and insect wires   zinging
                        they swallow a droplet of night.

no data reported of your kind here not in these lowlands too wet too flooded
termite mounds grow to mausoleums   earth by muddy earth humidity code
of incorporeal transcribed

be enthusiastic   use superlatives
a smooth face flowing

jungle-huddled   shoal   grass   weep integrity   like black moss
oceanic statehood   bodies sank to sexual economies when armies
strangled lovers before using them up first in a burned salt barn

a refusal to awaken on
the part of the subject

who assassinated femme supremacy?
decide to un-fracture conquest of feminine ache   to live where border mobility
are biological manifestations

hypnotic patter maybe likened
to a brick wall

in alliance you were made to partner with deep softness

lettii-i-ing go-o-oo
so-o-o-o comfortable
loose
limp
heavy

                    once nautical nomadic people moored in cities like   new york   dubai
toronto   honolulu   geographies written between dance floor rim & portals of
                                                  a dappled isthmus   at depths

a garden of anthozoa and whale sonics   people cannot not reach
without capital or commerce

those unable to move at will surrender to a *graveyard silence* an
astrological aspect affirmed as midnight nears a peak of alteration

rice paddies sink to mid-heaven while fisherman in drag cha cha across
karaoke bars and microeconomy shops stringing their goods like *look at
our emeralds & see shadows* another pair of swinging plastic sandals in
formation

let us loop like a bowline   carve it down to a blunt tip
use its kohl to shield eyes   *let's show them what it means*
what it means to be   *a devastating biyuti*

[induction in self-loyalty]

1. hollow out a small patch of earth the width of a spinnaker

2. observe a pattern in the flood

3. become stone in a gale

4. dive as an albatross seizing food that sears where sap flowed

5. learn multiple rituals of femme audacity

6. abandon pretty in the arroyo

7. seize desire without others

8. peel another layer of spectral radiance for every intimate question

9. allow each empty part to be driftwood

10. return in any order or fashion but honor the return

[escape from monkeyhouse]

we transform ourselves into
transparent mediums, fluid synthesis from and within anthropocene

we hold these dewy writing instruments close to heart spaces,
honor our tools as mechanisms of re-narration

beyond domination   we hear pedagogies within
                                                the utterance of florals

        evergreens pronounced as trumpet sound,

        generative bird play in the center of madrones,

        as cultural poetics as much as an affirmative will

bronze bodies arranged like rounded crowns rise
with flaring buckeyes and horse chestnuts

inside amber, an eagle-owl shapeshifts into a square-faced mountain wolf

      mahogany legs   half-chewed in battle

                                    by another wolf

fold knees and ankles on unamended soil
such as these terrestrial erotics
become demonstrations
of our intimacies
of interdependence

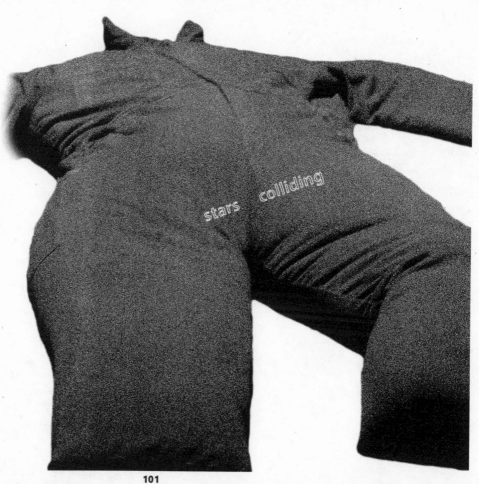

i blow smoke into your
one exposed ear so you
can feel my life force one
last time like intentional

stars colliding

101

[studies in becoming prayer]

alter   funerary
masks   to feral
address   feminine
gods of channeled
rage   adapt
consensual power

play dear lies
dear   sense&
pressure who hide
in this wool of
genitalia tangle

dear   ancestral
camouflage   of
strangler fig tree
limbs   to one
must bear witness

illustrations   integral to self-commitment   does
blood   not   deserve   cooperation&
reunion of tobacco

encrypted caricatures   preserved   to attachment
of scarcity   to its smoke   to its local shores
if not we are left   in (dis)contents of theatrics

document who survived after folklore
document (re)birth   document inherent magic by
locating theft of&from   those trees
how notions began   that there were none
document deconstruction   of high magic

we deserve to want hard as lamentation
love me love me love me   as scimitar
as blade flip as fast   as knuckle bone   as grove
as furrow as nothing short of

i chose to lay the rosary
beads down, companion
the sacred mysteries with
the ground.   commune
with birds

not   bird   as   domestic
companion,   bound   to   a
solitary   master   but
sovereign   being—
undomesticated,
unrepentant,
penetrating as fuck

i   look   for   high-soaring
night seers

through a smaller piece of
the defeathered flesh
of a weaker bird, i probe

what entities coerced me
to believe i adjacent to
a living thing of only
parallel or perpendicular
calibrations

*colonizer and colonized
have come to speak the
same   language . . . the
powerless have learned to
parrot the language*

*of the powerful. it all
depends on where you
stand and which side of the
scale is weighted*

tell me, wild bird, are you?

i was five when mother blamed
the bridge of my nose

                          underneath arch of my heel:
birthmark   seed   locus
                  ecology   red corals

disguised as my feet   my one
          blurry eye has intuition

like an archipelagic crone
circling a bowl
spiked fronds wielded

from blackbody radiation
even as foregrounds fade to
subjugation

mother says it needs to be
broken this nose knows

                envision church as archive of
occupation   arrowed a crevice of
nationhood   primitive hunt
            as punishment enclosed
by walls   why sumpter animals
      pull heavy chains   around
        a galaxy
            to be tamed

from plant to air to charcoal
what needs breaking   script in
      racist logic   metal chain
again metal rod

wind-   swept   leaves   messages
transport   signifying marks
insurgence upon settler colonial tar:

in another backseat of a white van
boys   and my skin lurches
they suspend   so   i   blade
sound   i wax fire   swallow   what's
left of heavens   to   protect
personhood   need   is

boundary   is touching   touch   this
left side of my shaved head
            & worship
                what i take down
still here   aligning talismans:

hawk-eagle   stippled feathers
talons of carnivores   swamp buffalo
cartilage   mother   this   face
knows broken   &soul-laughs
at composition

when someone's
white father shouts
family of monkeys . . .

to dismember
offer him his fingernail . . .

mice&mildew of fly paper . . .
sharp things . . .
slapping hands . . .

what death of your face
where men patronize

silence   what demands
trap us inside ourselves?

laws denying how I love
why a body blossoms
then expels

head down at the table
of your roasted meat

i permit myself
power to feed

[albularya]

they steep moringa and eucalyptus in an ochre cup &
present brackish burgundy lipstick   the tea they tell me

is for my famished body   lipstick to remind me that death
although marked in shade   is never monochrome

everything in their home smells of lauric oil   raffia palms
over the stove   i burn dried leaves of the molave

flies war around jars of palm jelly   canned vinegars sit atop a plastic table
my violent swats   their body rattles

spiders raid cupboards   crystalize to statuettes
betel nut on their tongue
            a song while painting my lips
            to sineguelas
            flesh of spanish plums   those spaniards had a thing
with those biblical harlots   the mirror glosses back
                  as i examine my stained teeth

above this hut bent   into fin to withstand typhoons
            there's a gigantic   but un-monumental star
            the air shifts:

            a pile of smoking garbage
            to burning molave leaves
            then back to star

end·lings

end·lings

1. The title of this book came to me on May 27, 2020, the month of George Floyd's murder and when Black Lives Matter-LA protesters converged shortly afterward in downtown Los Angeles. As demonstrators blocked the US 101 Hollywood freeway somewhere between Alameda Street and Aliso Street, I was a mile away with a book in hand, cross-legged atop a mountain rock. A caught a glimpse of a striped snake chasing a lizard into some shrubs, then the all-too-familiar sounds of helicopter blades circling above me and moving towards the city skyline. I was reading Cecilia Vicuña's poem, "The Quasar." The poem's original lines are: "Everyone knows what poetry is, but who can say it? / Its nature is to be felt but never apprehended." *Spit Temple: Selected Performances of Cecilia Vicuna*, (edited by and translated by Rosa Alcalá), Ugly Duckling Presse.

2. [mercy ceremony]
Some lines were borrowed and rearranged from Édouard Glissant's chapter "The Black Beach" from *Poetics of Relation* Relation (translated by Betsy Wing), University of Michigan Press.

3. [survivor's topography]
    "astral renegades" are words plucked from June Jordan's poem, "Queen Anne's Lace,"
    Things That I Do in the Dark: Selected Poems, Random House.

4. [letter to streets that burn you]
    Inspired and informed by the film, *Markova: Comfort Gay,* written by Clodualdo Del
    Mundo Jr. and directed by Gil Portes.

5. [on cures & abrasions from a responsive environment]
    "capitalism, having already found a way to turn profit on disaster" is abstracted
    from Aimee Bahng's chapter "Homeland Futurity: Speculations at the Border" from
    Migrant Futures: Decolonizing in Financial Times, Duke University Press.

6. The title for the second section is from Christine Borland, Ian Hunt, and Francis
    McKee's book, *Christine Borland: The Dead Teach the Living – Selected Works 1990-
    1999,* Migros Museum, Zürich. "The Dead Teach the Living" is an English translation
    from the Latin inscription "Mortui Vivo Docen" found on a wall from a dissection
    theatre of the anatomical institution. I'm unsure where, perhaps some university in
    Salamanca, Spain or Padova, Italy.

    This book is a catalog of the Scottish artist, Christine Borland's exhibitions that took place at de Appel in Holland, Migros Museum in Germany, and Museum Serralves in Portugal. Before my last day in Glasgow, I discovered Borland's candescent sculptures of heads mounted on plinth at the Kelvingrove Art Gallery and Museum. It was there that I saw one sculptured head of a man from Borneo and one from South Africa. There were many heads. One head was described to possess "Nordic features," yet I stood and lingered on the heads of African and Asian men. Their expressions had that glow of death's eternal sleep, but there was also a clinical feel in their shut eyelids and mouths. I was soon transported to a space of Western sciences, their historical involvement in biological racism, unauthorized autopsies, and medical experimentations…then a dream that I had the night before, one of ivory clouds as floating heads.

7. [transmitter signals when in proximity to power collapse]
    The line "how to not conjure the stones but threat itself" is inspired by "How do I not write about the stones but the heat itself?" from Eli Clare's *Exile and Pride: Disability, Queerness, and Liberation*, Duke University Press.

8. [ghosts in charged objects]
    "picture diary of a girl" was derived from the title of the book, *The Hidden Battle of Leyte: The Picture Diary of a Girl Taken by the Japanese Military* written by former Filipina comfort woman Remedios Felias, Bucong Bucung.

9.   [tattoo as softening ritual]
     Lines are borrowed and rearranged from "I Want This to Be True" by Jenny Boully, *The Georgia Review*, Winter 2020 Issue, and from "The Burned Sinner and Harmonious Angels" by Clarice Lispector, *The Complete Stories* (translated by Katrina Dodson), New Directions.

10. The title for the third section is from Rodrigo Toscano's "Re-opening a Poetics of Re-openings (A.K.A. 'Naked Strategic Partners')," from *Diasporic Avant-Gardes: Experimental Poetics and Cultural Displacement* (edited by Carrie Noland and Barrett Watten), Palgrave Macmillan.

11. [a girl too disenchanted to indulge in romantics]
     "obedient and defiant" was abstracted from the title of Portuguese artist, Paula Rego's first retrospective exhibition, "Obedience and Defiance" held in Europe (Scotland and Ireland). The title for the exhibition was a collaboration between Paula Rego and curator, Catherine Lampert. Rego states in an interview: "I'm interested in seeing things from the underdog's perspective. Usually that's a female perspective" (interview by Juliet Rix), *Studio International*, June 2019.

     For many years, I've been enamored by Rego's artwork. She continues to be one of my favorite European feminist painters. I return to her work when I want to revive my curiosities and perversions. In 2017, I traveled to Cascais in Portugal to visit Rego's Casa das Histórias. I stayed until the museum closed. Afterward, my brother and I did clumsy head stands and tumbled like children on the museum lawn under a maritime pine.

12. "ruffled skirts that that raise themselves (like phantom ship) on a sea of oil" was derived from Anne Garréta's *Sphinx* (translated by Emma Ramadan), Deep Vellum.

13. [cut an opening to mend the me]
"reimagination and subversion should be inherent in any Filipino work given our history. i am surprised when folks try to abide by the normative" is from an email written to me from the writer, Eileen Tabios.

14. "when trauma exposes the hybridity of the self, it exposes the multiple, often incompatible…through which we give meaning to what we live through" is abstracted from Joy Ladin's essay "Autobiography of a Hybrid Narrative: Finding a Form for Trauma" from *Family Resemblances: An Anthology and Exploration of 8 Hybrid Literary Genres* (edited by Marcela Sulak and Jacqueline Kolosov), Rose Metal Press.

15. "roots, stalks and trees…i have not yet as sung as i want….queer songs but as i grow older they will be queerer still" is from José García Villa's poem "Testament," from *Many Voices*, Philippine Book Guild. Here, other words are borrowed and reassembled from

an interview with the artists, Kim Anno, Jan Christian Bernabe, and Laura Kina. The entire interview is titled "Queer Traveler—on Desiring and Failing Sublime Landscape: An Interview with Kim Ano," published in *Queering Contemporary Asian American Art* (edited by Laura Kina and Christian Bernabe), University of Washington Press.

16. Other lines are abstracted and slightly reassembled from a letter-poem from Ruth Elynia S. Mabanglo's book, *Mga Liham Ni Pinay* (Letters of Pinay). I found translations of Mabanglo's letter-poems from Neferti X. M. Tadiar's chapter "Poetics of Filipina Export" from *Things Fall Away: Philippine Historical Experience and the Makings of Globalization*, Duke University Press.

17. "power of touch as both boundary and trespass" is from William Faulkner's Absalom, Absalom! I found it in Sharon Patricia Holland's *The Erotic Life of Racism*, Duke University Press.

18. [albularya]
The translation of this poem into Hilgaynon-Illongo was an intergenerational and matrilineal led collaboration with my mom and her friends, non-blood-related titas. This felt like an emotionally risky project because, although I was born in the Philippines, I've never been fluent in Hiligaynon. I'm not a scholar on Filipino

languages either. But this poem gave me reason to work with my ma creatively and uplift all the ways she is in community with others.

Hiligaynon is a Bisayan/Visayan language spoken predominantly in the Western Visayas region of the Philippines. Ilonggo, a dialect of Hiligaynon (also known as Siná) is spoken mostly in Iloilo City, the province of my birth. Ilonggo was then combined with the Hiligaynon language, often used when writing formal text and literature. In the Philippines, the two official languages spoken are English and Tagalog. I wanted to translate my work using the vocabulary and intonations of my family and our region. Like many first-generation Filipinx immigrants, there have been many personal experiences of language erasure and cultural amnesia. This poem was a small attempt to bridge these connections.

19. [contradictions in kinship]
"product of moonlight as much as sunlight" is derived from Bhanu Kapil's *Schizophrene*, Nightboat Books.

20. [keeper of blades]
"wicky-wacky-woo" are song lyrics from the Warner Brothers film *My Dream Is Yours* (1949). I watched parts of this film when I was a child in the Philippines. I

remember Doris Day sings this song dressed as a hula girl to imitate the hapa haole look Hollywood fetishized (and continues to fetishize) in the 1940s. Years later, I discovered the song was called "Nagasaki," written by Harry Wilson and Mort Dixon in 1928. This was referenced in a book I later read. *Empire's Mistress: Starring Isabel Rosario Cooper* by Vernadette Vicuña Gonzalez, Duke University Press.

21. [contradictions in kinship]
    I borrowed lines from the poem "Movement Song" by Audre Lorde from *The Collected Poems of Audre Lorde*, W. W. Norton & Company. Other sampled lines are from the poet Enriqueta Lunez and her trilingual book *New Moon, Luna Nueva, Yuminal Jme'tik* (translated by Clare Sullivan), Ugly Duckling Press, and the poem, "a reading from the book of the andes or the songs of indigenous scar" by Agustín Guambo from his bilingual book, *Andean Nuclear Spring* (translated by Carlos No), Ugly Duckling Presse.

22. "graveyard silence" is derived by James Baldwin's *Going to Meet the Man*, Vintage.

23. "look at our emeralds & see shadows" is derived from Alice Notley's "Book One" in *The Descent of Alette*, Penguin.

24. "let's show them what it means to be a devastating biyuti" is from a quote from Alder and possibly other Filipino gay men, abstracted from Martin F. Manalansan IV's

chapter "Locating the Diasporic Deviant/Diva" from *Global Divas: Filipino Gay Men in the Diaspora,* Duke University Press.

25. Other italicized phrases are part of a found poem I wrote from borrowed language from C. E. Cook and A. E. van Vogt's *Hypnotism Handbook,* Borden Publishing Co.

26. [transmitter signals from a young brown feminist]
Some fragments and rearrangements of fragments were inspired and abstracted from Jodinand Aguillon's essay "Hataw: Queer Choreography and the Routes of Diasporic Filipino-ness" *Diasporic Intimacies: Queer Filipinos and Canadian Imaginaries* (edited by Robert Diaz, Marissa Largo, and Fritz Pino), Northwestern University Press.

27. [amulet for a changing child]
The title is derived from the title of poem "The Amulet" by Ralph Waldo Emerson. The first few lines of Emerson's "Amulet" go like this: "Your picture smiles as first it smiled; / The ring you gave is still the same; / Your letters tells, O changing child! / No tidings *since* it came // Give me an amulet / That keeps intelligence with you . . . "

28. "the osprey with that cry" was borrowed from Derek Walcott's poem "Names" from *Collected Poems 1948-1984,* Farrar, Straus and Giroux.

29. "celestial placenta" was abstracted from a letter that Mexican Surrealist artist Remedios Varo wrote to her brother Dr. Rodrigo Varo about one of her paintings: *Microcosmos (or Determinismo)*. The letter can also be found in *Letters, Dreams & Other Writings* (translated by Margaret Carson), Wakefield Press.

29. [escape from monkey-house]
     "as cultural poetics as much as an affirmative will" is abstracted from Barrett Watten's "Hejinian's Ethics" from *Aerial 10: Lyn Hejinian* by Lyn Hejinian (edited by Rod Smith and Jen Hofer), Edge Books.

30. [studies in becoming prayer]
     "colonizer and colonized have come to speak the same language…the powerless have learned to parrot the language of the powerful. it all depends on where you stand and on which side of the scale is weighted" is from Trinh T. Minh-Ha's *Woman, Native, Other: Writing Postcoloniality and Feminism*, Indiana University Press.

acknowledgments

Many thanks to the editors of the following publications where individual works, excerpts, and/or earlier versions of these works have appeared: Academy of American Poets' Poem-a-Day Series, *Anomaly/ANMLY*, *Apogee Journal*, *Black Warrior Review*, *The California Journal of Poetics*, *Michigan Quarterly Review*, *Pleiades Magazine*, and anthologies *Liwanag 3* (a collaboration with SOMA Pilipinas and Kearney Street Workshop), and *Urgent Possibilities: Writings on Feminist Poetics & Emergent Pedagogies* (eohippus labs).

...

First and foremost, eternal thanks to my grandmothers, my lolas, Maria Luz Hinahon and Virginia Decena who are always watching over me. I see and understand all the times you were unable to speak or were made silent. I am grateful for your fire and sacred rage that lives in me and propels me forward.

To my dear family, my parents, Andy and Ivonne Peñaredondo, I've learned so much for your resiliency, stories and histories of snap and bounce-back. My unending gratitude to my brother, Anton Peñaredondo, who will always be one of my best friends and treasured allies in this lifetime. Your sibling love and camaraderie is an unforgettable gift.

To the constant mentorship of Allison Adelle Hedge Coke and Michael Jayme. Thank you both for your guidance and wisdom. Thank you for reminding me to trust in my creative visions and helping me to articulate them.

To the dedicated and hard-working editorial team of Noemi Press: Diana Arterian, Sarah Gzemski, Suzi F. Garcia, and Steve Halle. You were always there to read those very late-night correspondences of mine and respond with care and sensitivity. Diana, thank you for believing in my work and seeking me out so I could bring it forth here.

Many thanks to the literary arts and arts organizations that provided the time, space, community, and mentorship that aided the development of this book. To Kundiman and your labor of love that continues to bring together and forge so many wonderful writers, valued friendships, and communities. To the good folks of the Disquiet International Literary Program in Lisbon, Portugal and DISQUIET's post-program residency in São Miguel, Azores. To write, study, and create art and community abroad is a privilege, but is also enrichment to self-preservation as a writer. Thank you for giving me the opportunity to travel and write. To the Fine Arts Work Center in Provincetown who brought together Andrea Lawlor and our lovely queer group of fabulist lit writers.

So much of this book would not have been possible without the warm support, knowledgeable and generous exchanges, open conversations, precious space given to me by so many writers, artists, scholars, and collaborators who I admire very much: Tala Oliver Mateo, for your art, your stories, and your fierceness; Muriel Leung, who read the raw drafts of this book, still stuck by it and inspired the title "mercy ceremony;" Randa Jarrar, my Cap-twin of pleasure and pain, our nourishing ocean visits when the world sometimes goes dark; Kay Ulanday Barrett, for your unflinching light and leadership; Vanessa Angélica Villarreal, Vickie Vértiz, Janice Sapigao, Jason Magabo Perez, Rachelle Cruz, Kamala Puligandla, Addie Tsai, Ama Codjoe, Sally Wen Mao, Simon Shieh, Juan Morales, Craig Santos Perez, Don Mee Choi, Myung Mi Kim, No'u Revilla, Hari Alluri, MT Vallarta, Jen Eleana Hofer, Ronaldo V. Wilson, Andrea Abi-Karam, Marci Vogel, and Vidhu Aggarwal.

Glowing thank you to Susana Parras (and Miles too), for not only helping me finalize the title for this book but for also being a life raft and an extraordinary healer and friend who holds space for all my fiery, gooey parts. Thank you for teaching and showing me what anti-carceral, critical race, and harm reduction healing justice can look like in the community and inside ourselves (fist bumps with flowers).

Love and gratitude to Claudia Torres-Ambriz for their unwavering support, unfazed belief in me and my work, endearing punk ethos, and artistic vision and intellect that helped shape this book while I struggled and morphed with it. It was honor to revive your sculptural work, which became our creative collaboration within the pages of this book, an alchemy of my words and your images. I wish for us more future adventures, artmaking, mountain romps, dreamtime in the real time, survivance!

Offerings of gratitude to my ancestors, my diwatas, engkantos, and anitos. Offerings of gratitude and song to my queer and trans archipelagic ancestors and guides. Thank you for helping me to love and revere all my many, messy selves.

Thank You to Supporters of Our 2022 IndieGoGo Campaign at the $75+ Level

Jasminne Mendez

Roberto Tejada

Anthony Cody

Soham Patel

Ricardo Maldonado

Ada Limón

Eve Ewing

Francisco Aragón

Suzi F. Garcia

Ryan Kim

Heather Risher

Hannah Ensor

Vanessa Angélica Villarreal

Susan Briante

Tyler Meier

JD Pluecker

Leah Huizar

Divya Victor

Joshua Escobar

Sandra B. Greenstein

Ángel García

Jacob Daniel Ortiz

Nawal Nader-French

Grace Shuyi Liew

Michael Dowdy

M Soledad Caballero

Mary-Kim Arnold

Raquel Gutiérrez

Grisel Y. Acosta

Chloe Garcia Roberts

Eduardo C. Corral

José Olivarez

J Michael Martinez

Sarah Gzemski

Aichlee Bushnell

Ashaki M. Jackson

Victoria Chang

Jacob Daniel Ortiz

Gina Franco

Jacob Shores-Argüello

Michael Torres

Gary Dop